MEMOIR OF A

HOODSTA

Don't judge until you understand

By

Johnny Griffin Jr

Dedicated to my struggle.

I dedicate this book to my three sons—Marquise, Markell, and Johnny.

I hope they find their purpose.

Hopefully when it's not too late.

Table of Contents

DEFINITION OF A HOODSTA 7

THE DAY EVERYTHING CHANGED 12

LETTER TO MY SEEDS 73

AMERIKKKA 75

GONE 77

NFRNDS NO FRIENDS 79

HEAVEN FOR A HOODSTA 80

IMMORTAL 82

COLOR BLIND 84

LA COSA NOSTRA 85

JUDGE 87

SCARRED 89

UP 91

LIFE 93

ENOUGH 95

THE PROMISED LAND:SHORT ESSAY 97

GANG SH*T 100

SANITY 101

RIGGED 102

INDOCTRINATED 104

ILLUSION 105

GOT IT 107

NUMB 109

GOD DON'T LIVE HERE 111

SOULS MEET 112

DEAR BG 113

LETTER TO MOMS 115

WILLIE LYNCH SYNDROME 116

RICH 118

YOUR HEART 120

BIG BUSINESS 121

THESE STREETS 122

THE PLAN 124

THE GANG 125

ONE 127

THEY WONDER WHY 128

NOBODY 130

TINY SWEEZE AND CP 132

PUBLICITY STUNT 134

BACK IN THA DAY 135

HAMMERS & COKE 137

CATTLE 139

South Central Glossary 141

Author's contact.. 153

DEFINITION OF A HOODSTA

A resilient individual with character

and honor, who survives in trenches all

across the world, known as thy

neighborhood.

It was in 1992 when I first began riding shotgun with pain, backseat with misery like two childhood companions. I was eight years old, struggling to process why I was repeatedly sulking walking down a short flight of steps, headed toward my ill faith, on my way to fetching a switch like I was being groomed into slavery. During my brief walk, I was always stuck wondering what I had done so badly as a child that I deserved to be beaten. Even if I was being disobedient or rebelling in some way, at that age, that type of rearing still would be constituted as cruel.

I would stand at the tree knowing if I grabbed a slim stick compared to a fat one, I would indeed pay for it anyway. I was always left with picking the thicker branch. Normally, I was punished for being caught with food crumbs around my mouth—minuscule things of that nature. I'm pretty sure I was getting into regular kid mischief, nothing major.

In that stage of my life, everything I learned was by brute force, such as tying my shoes. Those hard lessons consisted of me being knocked in the head with whatever furniture ornament was near the mantel whenever I missed a swoop of the laces. My mother, who was in her late twenties then, was not the aggressor nor participated in my punishments. I don't recall her disciplining me, only yelling at times when she was not in a favorable mood. I couldn't understand then, she was rendered helpless in saving me from castigation, due to her own turmoil that she was imprisoned in daily.

Vikeetra Cross was fifteen years old young when she married my father, who was ten years her senior. My parents married in the middle of Aunt Bobbie's living room, with my granny's permission. From what elders have shared with me, that's how it was back in their day.

I was never caught by my mom doing whatever crime I was being accused of then. Most of the time, I was snitched on by the dude's niece, whom I had grown to despise. The truth of the matter was, if I wasn't deprived of food, I wouldn't have had to sneak it, which was mainly what I was always being punished for.

All the chaos that took place in my young existence was around the time of the well-known publicized Rodney King riot, which will forever be documented in history as one of the most controversial race riots in history. One specific time, Fatboy and his crime partner had come up with a bunch of merchandise from the looting they partook in the night before. News channels projected several days of blacks running around the ghettos of Los Angeles like savage animals, stealing and committing arson. More than fifty people were killed along with over 2,000 individuals injured.

I woke up the next morning, covered in brand-new clothes on a dirty beige couch that I shared with my big sister, Bunikie, whom everyone in the family called

Nikie. I'm not sure if it was from the sunrise gleaming in from outside, or if it was the blanket of clothes I was smothered in that woke me. Once I got the sleep outta my eyes, I noticed boxes of remote-control cars stacked high in the middle of the living room. I remember thinking, *I know for sure I have one of these toys coming.* I never received one. That wasn't the worst of things. The thug—who was more like my mother's captive—kept a variety of candy and snacks, just like the local liquor stores. He even had the clear buckets of red licorice that sat on the counters. When he was in a good mood, which was rare, he would give me and Nikie sandwich bags full of candy like it was some kinda allowance or reward. Those moments were always short-lived.

I was sitting on the couch one of many gloomy days in the living room watching television. Fatboy stormed into the living room like an angry grizzly bear, screaming, "You been sneaking and eating my shit, huh!" Sweat ran down his reddish butter-brown face, his hair scattered in a frenzy like a wild lion mane. He was infuriated with me like I had just slapped fire from his face. I couldn't comprehend what he was saying. He held several candy bars high in his hand that looked like they had been nibbled on daily by rats. He screamed away while I stared in shock, knowing I had nothing to do with those half-eaten Snickers bars I was sure to be punished for. I was getting blamed like I was the only person residing in the house.

My mother ended up with a monster shortly after departing with my father—a toxic rebound that sent her spiraling down a path of addiction, battery, and everything else a horrible relationship consists of. I'm not saying my father was God-sent from heaven to my helpless mother. He had his problems, shortcomings, and flaws the same as any other man walking this earth … probably one or two more problems than usual. I'm pretty sure she could give a more precise account of her husband's failures in marriage and fatherhood.

THE DAY EVERYTHING CHANGED

I was home alone in the front yard, playing, doing stuff that little lost boys do when bored. I was digging in the yard with a shovel until I burst a pipe that sent water gushing high in the open air like a fire hydrant. All I could do was stand there, gazing in the sky at the stream of water shooting out, scared, knowing I was in trouble.

A longtime friend of my father, whom I called Uncle Greg, coincidentally appeared, walking up from the sidewalk. To this day, I can't recall where he came from. I can't even remember if he stayed nearby. He talked to me for a while, asking questions about how and why water was going wild in the air.

After my brief talk, I went into the house not feeling better at all about my situation. I sat on the couch feeling nervous, visualizing what I had coming when my mama and my worst nightmare returned home.

God had finally answered my prayers.

I heard a car pull up abruptly outside. My head snapped upward from my lap, seeing my granny's canary-yellow Cadillac sitting at the curb. Then, my attention shot straight to my father, strutting hard, really determined, toward the door. It was like a new energy had formed over my scrawny body. I jumped up, ecstatic, thinking, *Nigga, where you been at? What took you so long?* I couldn't remember how long he had been absent from my life around that time. It didn't matter; the only thing that mattered to me at that moment was he was there when I needed him.

My daddy burst through the door like the long-lost savior I had been prophesying, immediately snatching me up in his grasp, and leading me outside.

Before that day, there were several indications and isolated incidents concerning my abuse that my family chose to downplay and ignore. My sister as well, which didn't last long due to the fact that my Aunt Ginger, who had several daughters, came and rescued her.

I'm unsure what propelled the decision for my father and grandmother to come and rescue me that day. The fractured boy buried deep inside me yearns to know in adulthood: Why did I have to suffer all those months and days? Why was I forced to endure all that physical and mental pain? I'm not speaking in the sense of ungratefulness, more in the state of wondering for my own mental storage.

After being whisked away like I was being freed from a refugee camp, I was taken to the closest police station. I guess my dad was attempting to file some type of child-abuse report on my behalf.

As a seasoned man with three sons of my own. I feel someone should have been filing a police report on my father for assault, or for the murder of my mother's boyfriend. These are just my eternal feelings. Who's to say if the act was ever committed or attempted? Honestly, I can't … I highly doubt it.

At the station, I went to use the restroom. Using the urinal next to me was an officer. I don't know what made this white man look down at a little black boy peeing, but I'm glad he did. Who's to say how long my suffering would have gone on before being discovered? He noticed blood in my urine. The policeman picked me up, carrying me back to the front lobby. You know how in life there are some things you can't forget? For me, it was that same officer reprimanding my father, in the middle of the floor at the station. "Instead of bringing him here, you need to be taking this boy to the hospital!" I was transferred back to the arms of my father and on my way out the door once again.

The end result was my mother, whom I love and cherish dearly, losing her three children, including me. I was admitted to Martin Luther King Jr. Hospital for internal bleeding from the beatings I received at the hands of my mother's boyfriend.

After my release from the hospital, Aunt Bobbie (*the monarch sister of my mother's side of the family*) was awarded custody of me and Nikie, who was already living there upon my arrival. Years down the line, Aunt Bobbie adopted my baby sister Vonnie from foster care, who was only a toddler then. Aunt Bobbie and Uncle Melvin took care of us along with their other two children.

My time at "Killer King", what the Martin Luther King hospital was coined by the ghetto in that era, wasn't all that bad. Just like the troublesome youngster J-Rock, in the old-school movie, *South Central,* directed by Stephen Milburn Anderson.

I learned how to play ping-pong amongst staff and ill peers, which turned into a favorite pastime of mine. There was even a female nurse who had grown quite fond of me. She went out of her way to find some cool pajama pants for me, so I wouldn't have to walk around the infirmary with my rear end on display from the typical tight hospital gown that opens from the back. I was thankful. Even for all the Carl's Jr. meals she would sneak in for me.

This was three decades back. Some memories are foggy; others appear clearer than a ship in the sea emerging out of a strong mist of murky clouds. Like the visual of my mother and father arguing at the front entrance of my hospital room, spewing cruel epithets and accusations at each other of who was at fault for my condition, while I lay on my stomach with a "swollen-ass" watching my parents act like natural fools. The two caused so much raucous, security was forced to intervene, resulting in L.A.P.D. being called.

After being interrogated by the officers, I went over several accounts of my abuse the best way a scared and hurt little boy could. From my recollection of that day, no justice was served on my behalf. Just my father's name being run through the law database, resulting in him going to jail and being stripped out of me and my big sister's lives for years to come.

Little did I know at the time, retribution would come in another way to my abuser years later.

I always vowed as a child to kill Fatboy once I was strong enough as a man. I finally got the chance—I thought—in 2006, right before I made my debut at a California correctional facility.

It was a typical Wednesday night in the one-bedroom apartment on Brynhurst Ave I shared with my then girlfriend Bre, before she became the mother of my youngest son Johnny. I was sitting on the sofa smoking a blunt consumed in my thoughts, chopping up work on a plate on top of the glass coffee table, when I heard knocks at the door. I opened the door, coming face-to-face with Bunikie, who had a look of uncertainty on her face disguised as a smile. After exchanging pleasantries, we made our way to the sofa where we sat. Immediately she began to run down to me how she had just run into Fatboy on the east side of Central, roaming the area near where I once stayed. Everything else that came out of her mouth after revealing that information fell on deaf ears. Instantly, my devious psyche began to form a plan of homicide. Unknowing to my sister then, she would be an accessory to murder. I sat there, pleading, doing my best to persuade her to drive me over to where the man was at who had caused me so much torment in my young life, to take me to the man who may hold sole blame for shaping my mentality negatively, constantly being in survivor mode, altering my perspective and fulfillment of living a positive life.

No matter how much I tried convincing her that I just wanted to have a talk with him, she wasn't going for it. Nikie knew me, and she knew if I got anywhere near that man, I would kill him. God had a different plan.

Centinela state penitentiary 2007 ... I was a couple of months shy of my twenty-second birthday. I was stuck in the cell on lockdown on 3 yard for ten months, with a friend of mine named Rodrick, or Baby S-born, whom I had known for years prior; he was more like family to me.

We were sitting in a cell watching television in a space that was the same size as a small bathroom when the correctional officer passed by, sliding mail under the steel door. It was a letter from my mom. It started off with, "You may be happy to hear this! Fatboy was found dead in a backyard, in the dirt, with maggots and ants consuming his whole body."

I can't recall being as heated as I was that day, after reading that letter. Hell naw I wasn't happy. I remember thinking, *I wished for nothing more than him seeing my face before he took his last breath.* I guess a slower death was more suitable for karma.

I had no real set destination when I first began my journey of composing. No master scheme; just a strong admiration for the art of literature.

I recognized my attraction to wordplay as early as elementary. I fell right in love with classics: authors such as Langston Hughes; books such as *The Rose that Grew from Concrete* by Maya Angelou, and even Tupac's version, which was my favorite; *Tortoise and the Hair; The Alchemist* just to name a few.

I enjoyed spelling contests that would take place on Fridays in class, right before school ended. I've always been one of those strong critics, critiquing a book thoroughly before finishing the following paragraph, looking for inconsistencies, figuring I recognized the plot off top, and always feeling I could craft a better version of whatever book I was reading.

My style has always been what I considered unorthodox. In my early adolescent years, around the time after my father was released from prison, I began to stumble across my talent.

My father, Johnny Griffin Sr., had retained custody of me and my sister Bunikie. I assume he was attempting to establish our lives back in the right perspective after the dismantling of our family, aiming to correct the past. His heart was in the right place in my belief, just not enough drive in his fight for reasons I would fail to understand fully until reaching manhood.

Like any young boy, I used to rummage through my father's belongings, searching his possessions, curious to learn who he was, eager to find signs of what had sculpted him into the man he'd become. As a kid, I was oblivious to realizing I had indeed discovered his Achilles' heel, rendering him incapable of being a good daddy—a homemade pipe stashed in his shoebox. If I was forced to be honest, it crumbled the solid perspective an impressionable kid had toward the man he once viewed as his solid hero.

Before I began my troublesome path, running through South Los Angeles as a reckless adolescent, thuggin' around gang-infested blocks, my idol time was spent in my room with the door shut, writing raps. Way before I was playing with .32s and .38 pistols, I was standing in the middle of my room, entranced in a fairytale world, clutching an invisible microphone like I was captivating a sold-out stadium, portraying a solo Westside Connection rocking the stage. When I first memorized Ice Cube's track "Ghetto Vet", word for word, that was a great accomplishment for me. I envisioned myself many years ago, sitting on the sectional with Oprah, chatting away, catching the twinkle of glee in her eyes while congratulating me on the success of becoming a well-known published author who had captured the people's ear. Even though the days of the billionaire lady who gave away houses and cars on her daytime show are long gone, I've always envisioned myself reaching high goals.

I would create full songs from scratch, straight a cappella, emulating Dr. Dre. Now, when I think back on my brief freestyle career, my amateur rhymes were decent enough. If I had kept pursuing and perfecting my rap craft, with some positive strong influence fueling me, I could have done numbers like a young Bow Wow, or even been in movies like Lil Romeo. I had semi-connections with Jayo Felony, so I could have gotten in the studio if I was serious enough. Key word: serious. Something I wasn't.

For those not familiar with Jayo, also known as Bullet Loco, he's a rapper from San Diego Rollin 40's Neighborhood Crips who was signed to Deaf Jam

Recordings in the early 2000s. He peaked around *1998* with a Cali banger "*Whatcha Gonna Do*" at the time when the Cali rap scene was repping strong.

This was about the third time I was back living with my father—this time in the heart of the Neighborhood Rollin 20 Bloods set.

The 20s had a strong reputation for beefing with nothing but Crips. Their territory was mainly surrounded by all Crips, and Bloods instinctively feuded. Some blood hoods were known to show sympathy toward Crips who they caught out of bounds, slipping in their territory, who were not close rivals.

Most of the time, my father's mood was always cold and unpredictable. He kept to himself, isolated with his troubles and away from me and my big sis, who had also rejoined the household. I briefly shared a room with her before she ran away from of our dad's controlling ways. Unable to deal with his unpredictable mood swings anymore, she reunited with our mother and found a home with her. Don't get me wrong, it wasn't all bad living with Pops. There were memorable times we shared when he was in a good mood, sober, and with a couple of dollars in his pocket. I've always felt he wasn't as invested in his kids as a father should be, with a young son growing up in South Central struggling to find himself. Simple fundamentals a boy receives from his father, such as understanding female nature or typical information, I received from the wisdom and philosophy of older associates who were titled "big homies" as far as the realms of gang politics are concerned. I gathered the essential fundamentals one must have to serve in the streets while serving stints in county jail. My criminal education furthered down the line in my hectic travels, graduating to state prison where my knowledge of ignorance increased—along with my barbaric mentality.

One random day, I had an opportunity to get out of the cramped apartment with my disgruntled pops.

My big bro Diece, who was my father's oldest son from a past relationship, told me he and Bullet were on their way to Chino Hills California to Snoop Dogg's house, to record some music. This was the beginning of the dramatized "Y2K hysteria" that was headlining all the news channels around then. I was fifteen years young and banged out. Any young Crip would have loved to meet the legendary "Murder Was the Case" rapper.

When the anticipated moment came, it was far from what a young loc such as myself would have expected. Diece and I sat uncomfortably in Snoop's cold-azz garage for hours with some random dudes that were hanging around before our arrival, while Jayo and Snoop were in the studio nearby knocking out their infamous track "Got Beef," which featured on the first Eastsidaz album. After hours of sitting bored and frustrated, I got up and began my adventure around the huge-sized house.

I walked around Snoop's mansion for about an hour, hoping to bump into him or anybody famous. What I remember most about his house was the sofas being wrapped in plastic where you would slide down if you attempted to sit on them. He had awards framed in glass in another room. Instead of hanging up, they were on the floor, leaning against the wall like he was moving or in the middle of decorating.

After taking a mini field trip in the massive home, the one that was on MTV Cribs years back with the

Lakers court in the backyard, I finally spotted him in the kitchen. Twenty years later, I can still remember what the Dogg was wearing: a leather Steeler-yellow NFL jacket with logo patches—the ones everybody was rockin' around that time. No disrespect intended, but Snoop had the tightest blue pair of khakis I've witnessed; this was way before the skinny-jean era. No shade to Snoop. I forgot to mention that he sported a blue bandana tied around his neck soulja-style, standing at the refrigerator knocking down a glass of Sprite. I stood less than ten feet away, staring his way, wondering if he could see me through the bottom of his glass. I acknowledged him with a head nod, letting him know I saw him returning back. To this day. I'm unsure what I was expecting him to say to a kid he didn't know. I turned around and headed back to the cold dungeon to post with my brother.

Though my long-awaited encounter with the West Coast pioneer didn't turn out like how I envisioned, nevertheless, I appreciated the memories. Who could say they kicked it at Snoop's house while history was being made?

After millions of failed attempts in my bathroom mirror, dreaming I was performing in front of a sold-out concert, sadly, I accepted the blatant fact that I wouldn't be the next Tupac Shakur. The stage scenery and all that came with it was not the monster I craved. The pen was my poison. I would say strong insecurities from a vicious speech impediment as a kid damaged my confidence severely, derailing me in ways a confused child was unable to grasp.

My speech problem was so bad that completing a sentence was an obstacle for me. If you are not a person who stutters, even the slightest, it's impossible to understand the emotions of a kid in the Los Angeles County school system, unable to get his name out at an attendance call. The feeling was like being stuck in the middle of a twelve-foot swimming pool circled by hungry sharks.

I was always considered a handsome kid with natural charisma. When your shoes had Payless on them instead of the famous Mike Jordan symbol while you were walking to what kids coined *stuttering class,* you were an easy target for cruel kids. I was even the boy whose ghetto auntie showed up unannounced, walking into the class with a loud housecoat, rollers, and belt in her hand, then taking a seat in the back of class, crossing her arms, and taunting me with her evil glare. The real-life Madea. Rest in peace to my Aunt Bobbie.

I say this to say, I wore embarrassment like a light book bag.

The first time I committed to taking a serious interest in reading was in 2004. "B-More Careful" by Shannon Holmes—the first book that actually inspired me to wanna write a novel when I was eighteen years old in the county jail for violating camp furlough.

For the millennials who don't know what furlough is, Probation had a program that released juveniles sixty days before their actual release date with strict conditions. If violated, you found yourself back in the same metal cot one previously left. Or at a new camp, depending on space.

I turned eighteen years old while in custody, which being in custody with a release date after your birthday was not an uncommon thing. I remember this Blood dude named Lil Boldy from Six-Deuce Brims who had a lot of the kids at the camp intimidated, based on his chunky size and age. He was nearing his twentieth birthday. How did he remain in juvenile custody that long? Anyone's guess would be as good as mine. He was the oldest, who was bullying the majority of the young Neighborhood Crips there. Once I had returned, his schoolyard tactics had deceased. I fought him to make my alpha status clear. Not long ago, I heard my juvenile adversary, Lil Boldy, had been murdered several years back.

I was sent to Los Angeles County Jail, where I served out the duration of my short sentence. Afterward, I was released back into the bowels of a hazardous society.

I was so deeply intertwined in gang activity on the streets, that I only got the chance to indulge in literature when I was locked up. Even then, all academics would take a back seat to bangin', especially when one belonged to a hated street gang—not meant to glorify—such as Rollin' 60s Neighborhood Crips. Fights mixed with jailhouse bullshit were constant.

I will rewind back to what landed me my first time in county jail.

A handful of us Neighborhood Crips fled on short notice to Birmingham, Alabama with a half-cooked plan of robbing a bank.

Someone, who was considered a respected homie at the time, who will remain anonymous, had established himself discreetly in the South. He rolled up one night at Victoria Ave. in front of the apartment building I lived in and asked those of us present, "Who wants to go outta town?"

We all had the mindsets of what the iconic film "Menace to Society" was built on; we all shared the ways of O-dog and Kane. We were young, black, reckless, and didn't give a fuck! All it took was a short conversation with me, Chopper, Tiny Tadpole, and another homie named Hansom, to be convinced to take the trip based on a police helicopter being non-existent in Birmingham. While we were on our way, what struck me as odd that day, was the conversation I had with my little buddy Marquise before we departed for out of town. He asked all of us, "Would you get my name tatted if I got flipped?" Though confused, I assured him I would, if the unfortunate ever occurred, tattoo his name on me.

There was nothing unusual about Marquise's request. In gang culture, death is common, even expected. What disturbed me the most was that I felt he was prophesying his future.

We rode the Greyhound for three days straight, stopping and letting our Nikes hit every piece of unfamiliar territory the Greyhound docked at. We clowned, having fun at all the stops in Texas and the whole way there. We chain-smoked menthol Newports like it was nobody's business. Every time we would reload the bus, passengers frowned as we passed, holding their noses, mad at the potent stench of marijuana that trailed us heavy like train smoke. We were around eighteen to twenty years old, highly active gang members, fresh off Brynhurst Ave, happy to be escaping the war zone of South Los Angeles we claimed as home.

After a short time living down south, things didn't go as planned. The vacation was short-lived. We got the news that our friend, Raymond Lilly, a.k.a. Lil Cappella, was gunned down within inches of his life, stretched out over apartment steps by the hands of a 77th gang-detail officer, forcing two of us to return.

We arrived back in South Central LA.

Chopper and I hopped off the Greyhound, not knowing what the days ahead had in store for us. We were back in the war zone we knew as home with a new problem already waiting for us.

Before parting ways, we exchanged hugs and locked in plans of meeting up again soon in the hood. After leaving the Greyhound station, I walked up to even more devastating news.

March 23, 2003 was a somber Sunday.

I was making my way on the Metro bus at the Avalon train station, located on the eastside of Los Angeles when I stepped onto the bus, bumping into a familiar face. "Did you hear what happened to my cousin, Marquise, like fifteen minutes ago?" asked Brenton.

I had gone months without speaking to anybody the whole time I was out of town, not even my mother and big sister. After vaguely hearing what he said, I stood stiff, then quickly shrugged it off. I stepped past him, making my way onto the bus, parting through bodies, thinking he had to be talking about someone else who was also a close associate and shared the same name. I stepped all the way to the back, not fully processing the words that had come from his mouth. After flopping down on the closest available spot, I let out a nerve-piercing wail that shocked the bus full of passengers. People stared at me like I had lost my sanity. In a way … I had.

The whole ride I rocked in my seat, holding onto faith that my young partner was alive; the man-child I had come to love like the bad little brother he had become. I held on to all doubt of him being dead. When the bus neared Crenshaw and Florence, while at the red light, a grim feeling overtook me. I noticed the helicopters near Slauson Ave five lights down hovering over the shopping center where Ralph's grocery store once was, as my faith began to trickle. I got off a couple of stops down in stride to my mother's apartment building.

I dragged down Hyde Park sluggishly, dreading every step I took. I could feel the eerie vibe of the leary streets sticking to my skin like garbage funk. It felt like a storm was near.

The first people I saw once stepping into the driveway was my fourteen-year-old friend, Marquise, and his mother and aunt—Shelly and Sheila. They were crying their eyes out, holding each other in the middle of the driveway. One of my homies named Crusty was standing at the gate with his chin to his chest. He told me how Marquise had been shot in his head, along with Crusty's twelve-year-old little brother Courtney who was blasted in his face by a kid himself who was fifteen years of age. He continued to explain how the two were supposed to pick up some ice cream for a birthday party but deviated from the task. As a result, young Marquise Pickens' life was taken by a rival gang member who lived in the same area but was considered out of bounds. He had been ordered to the store by his father, who was ignorant of the reality of gang politics when involving territory.

The year after Marquise died, Lil Cappella was killed. The three of us resided in the same apartment building on Victoria Ave before they were both tragically murdered.

The day Lil Cappella was killed, a group of members of the community were hanging out on 63rd St. between Brynhurst Ave. and Victoria Ave on a July afternoon. We were gathered around Raymond, who was seated on the porch, having a cordial conversation. He asked me if he could borrow twenty dollars, which I did have but refused to give to him for selfish reasons of my own. My hesitation to cough over the money was not intended to be such. I remember having a plan to re-up—buy more dope. I had a prime-colored Chevy Caprice with one front headlight, which was an '87 or '89—I vaguely recall. Well, it got snatched up by the police for lack of registration and I was doing my best to get it out of the impound. Surrendering the small amount of change he was asking for would have threatened my plan tremendously. Whoever has sold drugs on a small scale can contest the expression, "Every dollar counts."

Chopper pulled up in his baby mama's black Benz bumping Destiny's Child "Cater 2 U", screaming out the window that he was headed to the store to get some blunts. I got up from the porch and got in the passenger seat. Soon after we left, Chopper stopped abruptly, pressing down hard on the brakes in the middle of Brynhurst Ave. He turned back around, both of us forgetting to secure Lil Cappella by bringing him along with us due to the fact he was wearing a colostomy bag after being shot by the LAPD eight months prior. But, we were too late. Seconds after we reached him, the killers had already come through that fast, shooting several homies and killing our friend.

I held Lil Cappella's hand as he bled out on Big Ebony's porch, where he inhaled his last gulp of air. Where I witnessed a soul depart from a body; a death that will forever weigh heavy on my soul.

Right before his death, Lil Cappella had won a settlement against L.A.P.D. Rumor has it, the day of the incident, he fled with a firearm on foot which justified the officers—in their eyes, to open fire on him, injuring him severely. To my knowledge, a handgun was not recovered. I'm unsure if his mother received the settlement on behalf of her son before she sadly passed away years later.

The same officer went unpunished, rumor has it. Shortly after Raymond's demise, Officer Ross was promoted to homicide detective.

How do I make this brutal story short without sounding like a victim?

I've always accepted responsibility for my actions and the repercussions my decisions have brought me— good and bad. I was born in 1984. I have no proper education or diplomas, just a rap sheet long as a measuring tape, with a generation of dead friends that stretches about the same length. Most of my peers and friends have died from gunfire, and many are stuck with life in prison. I've been a victim of gun violence on several occasions.

In 2004, a few of my homies and I were standing outside early in the morning around eight o'clock when a green vehicle rounded the corner from Hyde Park Blvd, playing loud music. Off the top, I felt something was strange. Everybody present outside was on point, watching the approaching car. Baby CJ, who was killed years later, yelled out, "Watch that car!"

What had everyone hesitant to get on the defensive was the fact that music was bumping loudly from the car system, making us believe this was a familiar vehicle around the neighborhood. Anyone familiar with gang activity knows that's considered unusual behavior ... or a bold-tactical move. We would find out soon that it was evil coming to cause mass destruction to whoever was affiliated with the sector.

As soon as the car neared the apartments we were standing in front of, the passenger raised up from being seated, sat on the window sill, and began dumping shots. The assailant began discharging the assault rifle from the apartments beforehand. Around five or six of the tribe that were present, including myself, scattered for cover. Judging from the sounds of the loud fire power the weapon was giving off, whoever the killer was, was not playing.

My problem was, instead of taking off with everyone else down the driveway, toward the back where the garage was, I took off running with no firearm, stuck in the front yard with rapid gunfire flying between my body and over my head. I crouched down low, sprinting until I came to the end of a black iron gate where I had to lay down in the grass and fake dead. The same day, I learned a valuable lesson about sagging my pants.

The killers realized they had not hit any humans, just walls, gates, and trees; something that is unacceptable in gang culture, especially when bragging rights and rank were being challenged. I looked up, seeing brake lights flash, indicating the car was reversing. I jumped up with lightning speed, taking less than two seconds to pull my jeans up, turned around, and dashed back to the front. I had two choices: to cut left, take my chances running down the narrow driveway where I risked having my back eaten up by what sounded like a machine-gun upset; or I could have panicked by running out toward the street into gunfire.

I noticed my older homegirl, Tish. She had walked back toward the front, assuming the shooters had fled, oblivious to the fact they were backtracking in hot pursuit of murdering me. The gunman began blasting out the window like he was on the back of an off-road truck in Mexico, spraying with no regard for human life whatsoever. Seconds before the mean-green machine and bullets met me at the front of the driveway, I made it close enough to push her out of the way. In another swift motion, I spun around, landing flat on my stomach, facing the street. Immediately, I threw my hands over my head and started praying.

Shots flew past my skinny frame, knocking off the Seattle Mariner's cap I had been holding down on my head since the beginning of the drive-by. The 762s flew past my body as I lay exposed, screaming for God and my mother, who was nowhere around. I felt two shots at different times rip through my fresh Coogi sweater sleeve, ripping flesh off my arm.

I was behind a little azz bush that matched the size of an elf; it wouldn't be believed unless seen. I coined my spontaneous acrobatic skill the *I-don't-know-how-I-survived* move. After the bussing had stopped, I jumped up feeling like the luckiest person alive. Until I looked down at my arm that was burning then at Tish stretched on the ground. After coming to the undeniable realization that I was shot, I snatched my ruined sweater from around my neck. I looked at my mangled arm that had smoke coming from it and could see straight through my shredded flesh to my bone.

My big homie, Nono, came running from across the street to the rescue with a huge gun in his hand. The problem with that was, he was too late. He helped me wrap my arm up with the undershirt I wore underneath. I passed the criteria of being irresponsible at that stage in my adolescent career. From fear of having a warrant and possibly facing imprisonment from being shot while on probation, I was actually contemplating not going to the hospital. Before the foolish notion could gain momentum in my head, the ambulances were hollering in the middle of the street.

The paramedics approached me aggressively, attacking their duty of cutting my clothes off to identify any unknown wounds. I obliged them by taking my own pants off before they could play Scissorhands with them. I strutted to the transport in the front, half-naked, where I received a standing ovation from the whole block for being alive.

The medical staff at Daniel Freeman Hospital treated us like shit. Tish and I lost a lot of blood that day sitting in some kind of makeshift waiting area they had us stashed in. I didn't realize how scraped up and bruised I was until soreness began to soak in. I looked down at my arms and legs, seeing all kinds of gashes and scratches I accumulated from scrimmaging for my life. Tish's whole Achilles tendon was hanging to the ground which looked shredded, soaking the thick stack of pads the medical staff had enough decency to lay on the tile floor.

I found myself back in lockup in Jan 2015. The feeling of regret was different; more agony was attached. That specific term of imprisonment offered me a different hurt. The circumstances that surrounded my incarceration forced me to search deep within myself no matter how much I fought against doing so. I was sitting in a cold-azz cell in Delano reception. I'd received a three-year sentence—courtesy of being stupid, not counting the two extra years that ran consecutively that I was smacked with by the feds the day I stepped foot out the penitentiary for catching a case while on federal probation. That was handed down effortlessly from an old, disgruntled, shriveled up white judge, who I knew had no love for me whatsoever. One of the many downsides of the feds versus the state is that you're stuck with the same magistrate every time. I was back for the third time and was awarded two terms after less than a calendar year of marriage and freedom.

After my last release, I made the best attempt I knew how at that time of making a positive transition back into society. My fight would not have proven as difficult if I had the patience, support, and appreciation of my intimate family. Little did they know, their acceptance was what I was fighting for. What stung my chest like a thousand bees was the bold truth of the situation that led to my incarceration being nobody's fault but mine. Some things are better left unsaid. But, I will say this. I'm the fool who drove to the desert and picked up a snake then wondered why I was bitten.

I would never forget that day back in January 2015, the day I got locked up by the hands of my wife at the time. I was sitting at the 108th police station, cuffed to a hard log they called a bench, my head depressingly buried in my chest. I was beyond disgusted with myself. The anguish of my predicament strangled me further after using my free call to phone my mother.

"Mama ... I'm in jail!" were the words that coward above a whisper from my mouth.

"HOW IN THE FUCK YOU LET THAT HAPPEN, BOY? HOW IN THE FUCK YOU LET THAT BITCH PUT YOU BACK IN JAIL?"

was her response, with a few more vulgar words I care not to mention.

At that specific moment, I felt like the ten-minute tongue lashing my mother was whipping me with, was far worse than any verdict I could get. Just when I thought I was at the cusp of reestablishing and rehabilitating my life after being released from custody; just when I was trying to get things back in the right perspective with my two maturing sons and stepdaughter Mariyah, whom I accepted long ago and loved the same as my own children. Not to mention my youngest son, Johnny III, whom I was struggling to build a bond with. That's a whole complicated story alone. He was the result of a brief relationship I was involved in while separated from my then children's mother, who became my wife years later.

The majority of bitter females and vindictive women will not admit this. The scorned tend to cast their tainted emotions, birthed from the father's past discretions, onto their confused offspring. Subconsciously, that develops resentment and creates feelings of abandonment and mistrust in a fragile kid, whether or not the woman or kid is conscious of such harm. Exactly the difficult battle I had been forced to fight.

I moped on that cold bench all by my lonesome. I was back with a slew of bogus charges, a new gun case, three prior gun convictions, two prison priors, and I was just recently released from federal prison six months beforehand. Needless to say, I was fucked.

While I was wallowing in my pity, this slick-looking white man walked up to me.

"Hey, you from the 60s, huh? Do you know…?"

I veered in the direction of the voice, causing the metal cuff to clack hard against the steel bench. I stared at the unfamiliar man, confused, trying to process his angle. Before he snaked his way up behind me rambling, I was fully stuck in my head, contemplating all my problems I had coming up. The last thing I was trying to do was talk to anyone. He stepped toward me, then immediately invited himself to straddle the log like he had been anticipating the long-awaited moment. "Man, you're in a whole lotta trouble, ain't chu?"

I raised my head up and looked at this stereotypical white boy with his 70s-style salt-and-pepper combed-back hairdo. He reminded me of those hard-core bikers struggling to maintain their youthfulness. He appeared slicker than his hairstyle and was disguised in street clothes, attempting the civilian role. He started the convo off like we were long lost buddies getting acquainted, catching back up on old times in the neighborhood, with him being the one narrating the whole conversation.

I dropped my head back down to my lap with weight that felt like a brick sitting on my neck as I continuously shook my head. The strong possibility and almost certainty that I would be going back to prison wasn't even the heaviest burden on my back. I was unsure if buddy was trying to con me out of some information. That had me even more vexed than anything, the audacity of him thinking I would be that gullible and simple to turn. I'd been on that bus ride to the prison yard many times. It didn't scare me; I was seasoned to it. I would never be that down-and-out where I would sacrifice my soul to a devil. It was just the undeniable fact of guilt concerning my situation I was dealing with: I knew, I had fucked up bad. I was hoping my unresponsiveness was blatant knowledge of someone not wanting to be social. I really didn't care what the dude had to say. Don't get it twisted, the man did have a lot of intel, stuff he wasn't supposed to know. He was saying and was privy to a lot of inside information that couldn't have been obtained from any other source but from real gang members and criminals.

Starting as an adolescent, I've always experienced strange encounters, interactions, and conversations with random people on the LA metro transits, inside grocery stores, sidewalks, wherever. The things that the undercover detective was saying to me, left me speechless and with no other thoughts but, *I gotta put this in a book.* Though weird at times, every one of those strange exchanges revealed vital answers and information.

Shortly after, I plead guilty to a bogus assault charge. Seven months later, I was transferred from the county jail to the California Department of Corrections. Freddy Kruger's hideous face was not scary enough to describe the horrible nightmare I cast myself in that was indeed my reality. I was back at Delano reception with a fresh bid. I was nowhere at peace with my situation but overall thankful for my outcome. I had a handful of charges that could have put me on an extended vacation. On my first day in court, my public defender informed me I was looking at seventeen years off the top, with my then-wife planning to take the stand against me. He broke down to me how the authorities had all the evidence from the security cameras in the housing unit of me speeding out the projects in my 1992 white Lincoln Town Car like a fleeing bank robber down

Imperial Highway with my priors dragging heavily on the back bumper.

They had the surveillance footage from the Nickerson Gardens, her statements, and me throwing my weapon over the gate at Samuel Gompers Middle School.

I'm unsure if she was really going to take the stand against me. That's what my public defender warned me of at least, which was good enough to get me to cut a deal, quickly. There was no love left between me and my wife, then. So, if she was planning to take the stand to my detriment, it wouldn't have surprised me. While my court-appointed attorney was running down to me about how much trouble I was in on my first court date, I spaced out, thinking, *Damn, cold ain't even the word to describe this shit ... we just got married.* My wedding gift was my black azz being put back in custody.

In the beginning stages of my court battle, my faith was looking bleak. A couple of appearances later, things seemed to have changed somewhat in my favor on sentencing day, giving light to a dark thirty-six-month road ahead.

In reception, most of the time everyone is confined to their cell at a ratio of twenty-three to one. Meaning, you come out one hour a day for yard time, or recreation time. The next day is dayroom time for opposite tiers, where one can use the phone, shower, or whichever way one chooses to spend one's idle time. Some spent their lollygagging in front of their homeboy's cell, rapping about frivolous jail-house stuff, or getting caught up for a short time on what the others knew about the streets before getting arrested. I was too depressed to talk to anybody most of the time. All I wanted to do was sleep and dwell on all the mistakes I made after coming home from the feds. I was back, stuck in jail with nothing to my name, unable to see or talk to my kids. It was all bad in my world. I had no other choice but to soul search. In spite of all the emotional pain I was going through, I managed to maintain my tough-guy persona, which was a character I had sculpted and been working on since I was fifteen years of age, starting in the Los Padrinos Juvenile Detention Center.

When incarcerated, just like on the streets, everybody has problems nobody cares about. I walked the tiers and corridors with my head held high, feeling like everything was alright in my life, which was far from the truth. When I wasn't sleeping, I would hit the yard and work out relentlessly in the heat, doing pull-ups until my shoulders hurt, with a soldier standing guard nearby keeping watch for unforeseen threats. I had a reputation that carried from the Los Angeles streets and past stints amongst other things. I was notoriously known for my athletic escapades like running laps around the rec yards under smoldering heat conditions in work boots, which was bragged about by inmates as something like an urban myth. One time I ran sixty laps straight around Centinela State Prison's 3 yard in under two hours, receiving all the praise and acknowledgement from my cohorts.

When I wasn't doing strenuous calisthenics routines, I was reading anything I got my hands on— magazines, newspapers, it didn't matter. I would read some of the corniest literature ever written that I would have never picked up under different circumstances. Whoever had books in their cell, somehow, I became cordial with. I believe you can learn unconsciously just from breezing through a page or two. Those books kept me sane. No matter how down and out I grew with my stressful predicament, I remained me for the most part, laughing, somewhat joking with a few comrades here and there, critiquing all that I read relentlessly.

On the Delano reception yard, my second visit to Kern County is where I began constructing my first novel.

Three months later, I arrived at the old Folsom State Prison 3 yard mainline to begin my term. I was stuck on fish row—the tier for new inmates—for the first week with no money. I couldn't make a call until I was housed. I didn't even have enough for a stamp. I had lost a drastic amount of weight from sitting in reception. I had a cellmate named CJ from T-Zone Crip, who had food, and who also turned out to be a cool individual I would later connect with in society and do business with. CJ always made sure I didn't starve, but there was nothing like having your own commissary. No matter how giving or cool someone was, as a man, especially in prison, you gotta have your own shit: hygiene and food.

There is no way around it. No man can just scarf down another man's food like you would your own.

Fresh off fish row.

The only thing on my mind was figuring out how I was going to support myself financially. All the problems I had stacked on my plate was topped with bad luck. My newly discovered talent and ambition to write remained strong for the most part. When the whole prison population was on the yard doing whatever, I remained locked in my sweatbox, most of the time, studying the dictionary and any written material my creative writing coach, a distinguished man named Del Banjo, would bestow upon me regularly. His harsh authoritative British tone would nag me steadily, long after the hour-long class sessions we had most days of the week. *Make sure you read and write, Johnny!* rang through my head constantly. It was a mandatory obligation, and along with my mentor's stern instructions, I held it too religiously. I wrote at least ten pages daily, on top of reading diligently. There were days when I missed a meal and days when I had nothing, just books, pen, and paper.

The art of writing is a process that must first be conquered mentally. There's no other way around it. It takes steady up-at-night grueling, repetitive studying just to vaguely understand the intimacy it takes to interpret one's internal thoughts intellectually for another to judge. I'll be the first to admit, I've quit writing many times, relapsing shortly after. The brutal process alone of learning the art of writing is an honest testament in return, making me respect the craft and love it sincerely, something like an eternal admiration. There's always more to learn about this complex instrument. No matter the amount of times a story is heard or told, it's all about who tells it best.

May 2, 2018, was the day I completed a six-month halfway house program in El Monte, California, after finishing consecutive sentences in different jurisdictions.

I returned to society the same day as my middle son's, Markell, fourteenth birthday. After all the betrayal and disloyalty that I complained of in the previous chapter, I reconciled with my family. I was able to rationalize my decision with *Hey, it was all a part of my growth, all mistakes, flaws, big or small.*

I accumulated a bunch of material in my three-year hiatus. While in the re-entry home, I was fortunate to meet this good-natured man named Alex, who I let check out a project of mine on a random day I had started working early on while in custody.

Alex was a gentle soul whose salt-and-pepper hair I would cut often. I wasn't even that good at cutting hair of other races other than African Americans. Not that I'm prejudiced in doing so; that part of my barbering was not perfected then. For some reason, this stranger I had recently met had all the faith in the universe in me.

After that day, I arrived back at the halfway house after being out with my family the whole day on what the staff titled a day pass. After reading my work, Alex went out and brought me an HP Chromebook laptop, reprimanding me, saying how from there on out, I would have no excuses for not getting my writings out to the world.

Any person who has done a long stint of incarceration can contest the difficulties of transitioning back into society. It's a faceless demon that must be confronted. My biggest battle would be catering to regrets of being an absentee father the majority of my children's lives. Upon reflection, I'm able to dissect my past wrongs as a way of correcting my future decisions. I give credit to my setbacks and dilemmas; without such, I wouldn't have become the man I am today.

Shortly after my release and second-go-round of incompatibility called marriage, I was back in the streets heavy. We just couldn't get it right. The same problems that were there beforehand, progressed to a dense future.

I was a 34-year-old convicted felon with nothing but a jacked-up prison record with bullet holes and tattoos on federal probation. I was pitiful; I didn't own or possess anything of real value. A known gang member in South Central without a vehicle is equivalent to a man strolling through the lion's den draped in meat, smiling with no weapon. Just when I thought life was a female that couldn't get nastier, the unbelievable happened.

My mother and I were cruising down Fairfax Blvd, from out having brunch when I received the news from my lil homie, Tiny Shady Blue. I was slouched in the passenger seat of my mother's black suburban truck. I was already in a bad headspace from an incident that had me running for my life outta Palmdale around 3 a.m. that morning.

My mother was talking to me about something I was half listening to when she abruptly smashed down on her brakes inches from the corner. My mother is naturally a loud, animated woman. She spotted Guillermo Diaz crossing the street directly in front of us. I can't recall the name of the street we were on. My mother was beyond excited. She rolled down her window like she was suffocating, then began screaming out to him, real fanatic like. The moment was short-lived. In the middle of my mother praising the actor as the brilliant killer he portrayed in the hit TV show *Scandal*, I got a call from my young partner informing me that Nipsey had been shot six times, and it wasn't looking good for him. A gang is like a big dysfunctional family. Anytime anything transpired amongst members, there would always be someone to inform someone what had transpired. I shrugged it off, not taking the news too seriously. I guaranteed my lil homie that he would pull through, not truly believing any true harm had come to Nip. It was like, I half heard what he was saying without giving it validity. I had just talked to Nipsey two days prior. Even though I heard Tiny Shady Blue saying that Nip Hussle had just been gunned down in front of the Marathon store, my mind failed to fully process his words as being true.

Three days before Nipsey Hussle was murdered.

I was in Palmdale, California, where I lived at the time with my family. One night, I was visiting my friend C-Loc's clothing boutique, as I would any other day or time. We were hanging out inside the shop later than usual this particular night, way past city regulations for the store to legally be open.

It was creeping up at 2 a.m. We were listening to the *Crenshaw* album, getting super faded. For some reason, the album resonated with me more than other times, an album I've bumped countless times since its release. It affected me so spiritually in a way, where I had to pick up the phone and call him.

Just like Ermias' mother had stated at his home-going, Nip was answering more than usual right before his untimely passing.

"Hello ... what up nigga!" he responded energetically and upbeat like he was laid back on an exotic island somewhere getting blazed and enjoying the fruits of his labor.

We stayed on the phone with each other for about half an hour, rehashing past conversations and events, as his music played intuitively in the background of the shop as we talked. I did my best to articulate a masculine way to tell him how special and destined I felt he was, without sounding a way that could be taken as soft. Deep down. I already knew, he was a man of infinite understanding.

My intelligent friend understood what I was conveying to him, accepting my praise of him humbly in stride as he would do with almost everything. He laughed in the signature way he was known to, letting me know, the acknowledgement of him was accepted and appreciated, more based on who the compliment was coming from. We talked on the phone a little while longer, the little hand of the clock reaching the three. His last words to me were, "Don't forget to send me yo' book, Hood!" Little did I know, I had a long way to go before my story was complete.

It was a sunny Wednesday.

A couple of female friends and I were driving down Crenshaw Blvd with no set destination; the three of us lost in our own worries. We were rolling down a busy lane, consumed in frivolous banter when a weird energy swept over me. Right before we neared the mortuary, I noticed all types of fancy cars, squad cruisers, and police motorcycles parked around the perimeter of the funeral home, stationed in surrounding crevices. I wasn't that engaged in social media around that time meaning that I had no solid information about when the viewing or service would be, until stumbling upon the viewing that afternoon.

I instructed Tootie to park in the first available space inside Angelus Funeral Home. I was determined to see my homie. I didn't have any concrete evidence he was in there. My thoughts were, *Who else was big enough in Los Angeles at that time to have a fleet of luxury vehicles decorating the area with Muslims serving as security? Nipsey Hussle.*

I approached the side gate by the parking lot that faced Crenshaw Blvd. There were two Muslims at the gate who wore black suits. They were doing a good job from what I could see. Security was drilling a local singer named T-Fly with questions, refusing to let him in. He had collaborated with Nipsey on several songs and was doing his best at pleading his case before eventually getting in.

Instantly, they grilled me down with stone stares, assessing my rough appearance. The last thing I was worried about around that time was if I was fashionable or not. I was in a hoodie and sweats, straight grimy mode. The first words out of my mouth were, "Is my homeboy in there? I wanna see him … and no, I'm not on the list!" The two guards, who exchanged uncertain glances, both had different tablets in their hands and began scrolling for my name, which wasn't on the list. I wasn't worried about being allowed in or not. I was determined to get in, that's how serious it was. All it took was for me to catch the right person, someone like Black

Sam—his big brother. Seconds later, I noticed a familiar face: Adam, a man I had known for years, Nipsey's manager. After he noticed me going back and forth with security, he stepped up taking control of the situation, letting them know to let me through. I was good.

My heart began beating like a fist angrily trying to fight its way out of my chest, as I stepped inside the parking lot, making my way toward the mortuary's back doors.

The instrumental from Nipsey's *Mailbox Money* album "Overtime" blared low from the speakers into the dense atmosphere. Repeatedly following behind the melodic tone was "Blue Laces 2." The two songs coincided with a sad and gloomy mood.

I stood at the entrance disheveled, looking ahead at a man who was not supposed to be dead, in his casket. I dreaded every second of my wait, every step I took toward the viewing. Seeing Nipsey Hussle laid immaculately in his blue casket, under the opaque light, was like forcing me to believe and see something horrible that was not supposed to be true, was indeed real.

My turn came, and I stepped up hesitantly like some scared child who feared punishment. I placed my hand on top of his embalmed hand, which was warmer in comparison to the many bodies I'd seen and touched in the countless funerals I've unfortunately had to attend. The most experienced mortician could not have prepared him any better. His family had seen to it that he was put away like the king he was, dripped in jewels and all. Despite how perfect Nipsey appeared in his coffin, if there is such a thing, he appeared exactly as what he was—dead, a shell of his former self. He appeared as if he never possessed any life to begin with. His corpse resembled exactly how I felt: a good man robbed of his life, his kids forever robbed of the chance of basking in the glory of knowing and having a solid individual—their father.

During the time of my mourning, I talked to Nip, hoping he could hear me. I didn't care that I was holding up the long line. Out of nowhere, a hand firmly gripped my shoulder. I turned eye to eye to Jay-Z, saying, "I'm sorry for your loss." I could see the hurt in Jay's eyes as he saw in mine. He had a look buried deep in his sullen-socket's awoken eyes that said he wished there was something he could do, a magical way he could change this situation. In any other case, I would have been stoked outta my mind to be in Jay-Z's presence, talk to him, pick his brain, get any type of game I could get from him. Just not that day.

After I had the chance to reflect on the matter of Jigga being at the viewing that was more like a mini funeral, it magnified how special and worthy Nip actually was. It clarified how special people felt he really was.

I humbly accepted his condolences, shaking his hand before making my way out of the chapel before I lost the battle of breaking down crying.

On that tragic day, South Central depicted the *Ali* movie. The scene when Muhammad Ali was driving down the street, then erupted in pandemonium after finding out that Malcolm X was dead. That's how the Crenshaw-Hyde Park district reacted on March 31, 2019. A day I've still yet to fully process and accept.

Nipsey Hussle was the true definition of his name: a hustler; a go-getter. Even as an adolescent, to me, he always seemed like he had a plan. Even when he thought he didn't. He was always looking for a more lucrative income, always seeking to generate more money. If I had to take a keynote from a great man from all the years I knew him, it's that persistence does pay off—anything is possible. Nothing worth having will come without hard work and dedication. Most importantly, Nipsey's death screamed to me, *The streets can never love you. No matter what that person does or tries to do … no matter the amount of love one calls distributing back.* That's a fight I've yet to see won. I'm grateful to have known him, with a trunk full of memories to carry. His passing was a major blow to urban culture and black society. The marathon will continue.

The Grim Reaper was still prevalent at my community's door .

After the inconceivable fatality at the Marathon store, I found myself losing more friends as the days passed. I'm talking about the type of peers whom I knew their whole families on a first-name basis, and probably had brief flings with their sister or female relatives … those types of friends.

I was stuck in a toxic environment, fleeing from a failed toxic marriage. When I wasn't hopping back and forth from my mom's home in West Los Angeles and different women's homes, I was sleeping in an abandoned apartment building on West Blvd and 63rd St., where my gang had taken over by laying claim to. I mean, we didn't officially own the decaying building. We were a group of gang members illegally running a whole apartment building and not paying rent. We were leasing rooms with interviews and all. We weren't a New Jack City, but it was a mini replica.

When I wasn't hustling—selling drugs, I was smoking weed, getting higher than funeral services. I had so much anger knotted up in me from over the years, that the slightest of drama sent me through the roof. I continuously found myself in meaningless quarrels with associates and women. My relationship with my children was strained. I had returned back to an old lifestyle I had worked hard to get out of. I had no outlet, other than my eye sockets and pen.

The computer Alex had gifted me, along with all my personal possessions like clothing and shoes were taken, and my identification credentials were destroyed. What really put me in a bad head space and setback? I was purposely locked out of my Google account that stored all the work I had been working on for years— manuscripts I created while incarcerated. A small setback, nothing major. Nothing that could derail my plans of becoming a published author. I didn't allow that foul deliberate attempt to sabotage my dreams stop me. With roaches and rodents accompanying me in the dilapidated building, I rewrote most of my stuff with all-new material on my Samsung tablet. I typed with two fingers the whole way through, due to my finger skills being limited. My good friend, Lil Animal, accompanied me, stretched out asleep on the dirty couch next to me.

The moral of this manifesto that's far from over: I didn't let my troubled past and mistakes hinder me, hold me back, or discourage me from pursuing my talent—a gift that God has imprinted in me. I kept going … no matter what negatives or disadvantages existed. I've accumulated countless errors in the game of life. I've taken and have overcome losses both spiritually and physically. A true testament of resilience. The validation of a *Hoodsta.*

LETTER TO MY SEEDS

I understand baby's eyes are born closed to a

Certain degree

I still believe you're old enough to comprehend

Certain things, such as scandalous deeds like

Sneaking out at night

I'm sorry your daddy became a victim of

Something evil like

A scandalous dedicated cop working hard to have

Someone in a cell at night

Made it impossible for me to show y'all

The difference between wrong

The importance of doing right

Unable to embed in you

Slimy deeds always surface in the light

Or you can keep pretending

What that other parent does is right

I forgot, forgot to remember

That same person who continues to deceive you,

Satan, your true enemy

Is that same person that feeds you

All those lies served with fool's pie

All my incarcerated nights.

AMERIKKKA

The serpent used Eve to manipulate Adam

Sam got a new girl named Crystal, he uses now to

Seduce you

Her charm shines brighter than fool's gold them

Asians over priced you

Panhandling has become the black man's new

Profession

Brainwashing young black boys has become a

Bitter mamas' sole priority

In my hood, we numb

All this pain we transfer to guns

When black lives die, there's no reaction

We were taught to respond with rapid

Ammunition

75

We were never showed to raise the children

My older peers only showed us how to sell dope

And then pop the clip in

We never were told, you got more to live for

I only was shown, this what you was bred for

What else am I supposed to think when all I step

Out to is liquor stores

Gun stores around the corner 'cause in my streets

It's war

I guess that's what my reality was designed for

Imagine if there was a science center when I

Stepped out my front door

Instead of one of my distant brothers killing me

Just for taking a casual stroll to the store

Balloons and flowers decorate my corners

This is what *niggas* are known for.

GONE

Is tha days of

Standing on the block till sunrise

Rule was

Better have a gun glued to your thigh when

Enemies decide to slide

Traffic back-and-forth all through the hood till

Night time

Even tho a lot of death, still it was fun

Johnnie was code for "everybody run."

Homegirls used to carry our guns

We used their apartments to hide drugs and

Ourselves when on the run

One day I was sitting in my jail cell alone, all my

Commissaries gone

I realized this life just wasn't fulfilling anymore

I glanced left to right

No family around

Realizing all my friends are gone.

NFRNDS NO FRIENDS

I finally realize just like at the end

Right before that lone tear drops from your

Mama's eye

If you get that chance to gaze up in the sky

When everything replaying before your last cry

If you get that chance to ask why

When there's nowhere to hide

Nobody but the spirit to ask why

Only then at the end

You will realize

There will be no friends at the end

Like when you die

HEAVEN FOR A HOODSTA

I wonder if rebellious kids' past sins

Transgressions goes unforgiven

Will God forgive us for sinning, leading this

Lifestyle that we were given

Will he have mercy for those being religious

In

Violating the first commandment

Will he understand most of my role models

Were

Raised without fathers

They were tricked too

They were taught to administer bullets to

Their

Culture too

How else were they able to teach me how

To turn

Soft, hard

The importance of keeping a gun near the

Back

Door

Peace on Earth is something me and my

Peers

Never had the luxury of

When we go

Do we still get to see that place we only

Dream of?

IMMORTAL

I ponder where all the souls of past slaves

Migrated to

The drive of great kings of Egypt

Where did all that power fade to

My hand laid upon his

His embalmed corpse warmer than the

Usual

Incited second guessing is the truth really

Gone

Do legends truly live on

Do I possess untamed passion to carry on

Incorporated spirits are how greatness

Carries on

All that drive can't just wither on

All that style must flamboyant on

I'm just gonna keep pushing till another

Prophet

Is appointed

The marathon will continue.

COLOR BLIND

Look what Willie did to me

I'm fucked up

Why I think all black men are my enemy

Harming another black man is first nature

To me

My own is the only one bringing harm to me

When I approach a dark face I'm always on

Guard

Fear of a black man is why I stay armed

I'm aware of what Willie did to me

Still, I can't shake this taught animosity

I accept the menticide

My excuse is

Look what Willie did to me.

LA COSA NOSTRA

The teachings were cursed from the start

Who followed the rules was based on

Favoritism

From the start

Whoever would have knew

The same man you would have gave your

Shirt to

One of those bullets in his chamber is

Meant for

You

Big homies should have warned me

When you say you love me, that's code for

Betrayal

That's what made me

Menace to all society

This fucked up lil thing of ours

Been flawed from the start.

JUDGE

First you gotta face your mirror

Then put yourself in that hospital bed

Walk them same blocks as all my homies did

Watch childhood friend's mamas crying cuz

Their sons were shot in their heads

I'm talking about my homies that are dead

Have you ever been to state pen

Did you ever have to wonder if your kids were fed

Who was sleeping in yha girl's bed

Watch your back around childhood friends

Gave everything for yha kids and still ended

Up jailed, still got no credit at the end

Did you ever have to worry about eating

When you was a kid

All this shit

Is what had me facing a racist judge who

Sentenced me to federal penitentiary at age

Twenty-three

He showed the pedophile who got

Sentenced before me more leniency

Recidivism succeeds

I was paroled again at age thirty-three.

SCARRED

My photos consisted of colorful obituaries

Past memories I can't bury

Imprints on my stomping grounds they can never

Cover

Past sinful deeds to this day still hinders me

Last phone call I had with Tiny Shady still haunts

Me

Even that twenty dollar bill I didn't lend CP when

He asked me.

I still think about Lil Covette when she was killed

With baby Eddie boy

Last time I seen D-Mac, he told me I was special,

He just didn't know how to formulate it

Hittman told me he would die with my watch on,

Based on who gave it

All my niggas is dead

My nephew is dead

How can I not contemplate sliding

I guess we all die in the end

With all the wounds life opened from the crib

The question I ask

When it's time for my story to dead

Will it hurt at the end?

UP

This ain't no dream

Reminiscing over my dead homies when I'm

Supposed to be dreaming

Thinking 'bout all my niggas that got life

I know my hoodstas was guilty, we were never

Taught right

I think that's what encourages the nightmares at

Night

Watching childhood friends get murdered

Increases paranoia

This the kinda shit that keeps me up at night

More deaths adding to my paranoia

A treacherous snake got me contemplating

Moving out of California

Past mistakes and regrets I can't rest

After what happened to Nip, how can I not stress

If I'm next, I don't got no money for a vest

That don't even matter, these niggas takin'

Headshots, Homies treating their brothers like

Opps

Everybody acting like cops

When will this losing cycle stop

In this life we lead, we will never lead

I asked God for strength to leave the Rollin 60s

Before those same shovels bury me

To me, life on the block is equivalent to being

Stuck across in that same cemetery.

LIFE

All my friends are dead

Relationship with my sons share the same

Likeness

Cutting up rocks in spots is how I was raised to

Make profit

I stood up for count mad each and everyday

I held homies' hands, stared in their eyes when

They passed away

I was taught to put bullets in my clip then return

Fire

I used to cry about Tiny Sweeze everyday

I was standing in my cell at the door looking for

Mail most days

I felt like I was doing day for day when I was

Locked up in Victorville federal prison

I guess it's just life

When will mines begin?

ENOUGH

I been realized my love ain't enough

I guess it gotta come attached with two Brinks

Trucks

Couple of enemies' souls leaking between my

Fingers will never be enough

All my hungry nights on them cold metal bunks,

I still didn't get enough

I held Lil Cappella's hand while he bled out on

Ebony's porch

That 45 had his chest opened up

Lil Raymond dead wit a shit bag from when Ross'

Beretta ate 'em up

All this shit I gotta talk to God about

I might not make it up.

THE PROMISED LAND:SHORT ESSAY

As I grace the streets of Los Angeles regularly in transit, I find myself at a loss for an explanation as to why there is a drastic decline of black faces in urban communities such as South Central, Los Angeles. I quickly jar my consciousness back to the blatant truth. Steady black-on-black violence, combined with "murder by cop" of ethnic minorities are the leading factors of black extinction.

Tactics such as foreigners arriving with large currency, buying out struggling small businesses, monopolizing real estate, and in return, swaying the poorer class to take the fool's gold, being relocated to rural areas that strategically offer affordable living. A geographically designed plan that was put in formation way before 1966 when the Panther Party began. Poverty in every urban location is not by accident. Does that statement need any validation? Compare environments such as Beverly Hills and Culver City to sections such as the Hyde Park area located on the West side of South Los Angeles.

Trumped-up charges with astronomical sentences remain the leading tool of the government, to employ mass imprisonment on negros still, contributing to race alienation of African Americans. It is written that "an evil institution" ended 150 years ago, concerning African Blacks being counted-credited as ⅗ of a person. If that's not the case, why the random debate ever so often over reparations?

The masses will continue to deceive you into believing there has come a change in America in steps toward the process concerning racism, and the delegation of power to negroes.

Unexplainable tragedies in urban neighborhoods such as Nipsey Hussle's death in 2019 confirm that evil within self-taught hate is very much prevalent.

In my blurred eyes, the same circumstances that surround George Floyd will continue for years to come in my community.

Beforehand on June 10, 2016, Keith Bursey was murdered by cops on Slauson Ave and Brynhurst Ave. with no weapon being retrieved in regard to him from the scene.

The officer who killed him went unprosecuted due to justifiable homicide.

In South Central Los Angeles, where undocumented immigrants can obtain licenses, injustice, discrimination, and social caste have always been a reality for me and my peers.

A sad story of meaningless violence from demons created in 1619.

Way before the gruesome murder of Emmett Till. The treatment of Trayvon Martin still exists here.

GANG SH*T

When you dead and gone

They gone smear dirt on yha name

Do whatever they can to slander yha fame

How quick they are to forget all your sacrifices to

Earn yha name

Probably try to fuck on yha lil sister then yha girl

This is the price we pay for all this

Can't even be there for yha kids

Paid in full is all this

Take a bow

You can't from your grave

Behind all this gang shit.

SANITY

Lately, people have been proclaiming I'm crazy

I guess that comes with it

When the slandered voices his understanding

Somewhat of a more opened conscious

Most of the greats were converted into introverts

I guess that's coincidence

I guess nature just separates bird's view versus

Scavenger's thirst

Einstein was declared crazy by his peers, and

Relocated to special education class

In this sane world we live in

I'll choose to remain insane.

RIGGED

If I'm armed, I'mma shoot

Federal probation don't care

The state still gonna give me life if I shoot

What else I'm supposed to do

The same color in my mirror

Driving through filling me up with bullets if I

Don't shoot

South Los Angeles is very racial

Justice is only blind

When they see Africans, they shoot

Bias DA, you tell me what I'm supposed to do

I know your officers are trained to D.O.A.

If this was you

Would you want your mother crying her eyes out

Because she gotta bury you

I forgot

Blacks really don't matter to you.

INDOCTRINATED

When you wanna see your brother dead

Don't really care if your kids are fed

Praying your baby father get dead or jailed

Wishing the mother of your children fail

Spillin' black blood ain't the only way

Products of the same hood beefing on claimed

Corners

On the same street, how I'm standing with my

Enemy

Look what Willie did to me

Creation of evil made a hate-filled race

Now they use the 77th division to infiltrate

Autodidactic hate makes us eliminate.

ILLUSION

Who do you think you're fooling?

My vision is translucent

This potent marijuana I smoke has not diluted

My mind

I see it in the sky

I feel it sticking to my skin like a close enemy

Waiting for the right chance to dead me

I can't stand what society has declared what is

Considered real

You lie to me

I lie to you

Is the truth really dead

Something like love in the streets

Do you really think it ever existed there

Just like air

You feel it

Can never grab

Nor see it clear

I guess it's just something in the air

For tha aware.

GOT IT

Tainted DNA make it where we can't relate

Matter of fact

Keep yha backs facing me

There will be no snakes on the plane next to me

All of a sudden

You actin like you don't remember me

I guess I'm supposed to keep compromising my

Integrity

How do I expect closed eyes to see

All I can say

When you see me, you better act like you
remember me

I'll beat'chu up like you was born in 1983

I feel your energy

    You wanna be my enemy.

NUMB

When your heart don't beat no more

When you can't tell if you're capable of feeling

When you look both ways remembering all your

Friends are gone

When you realize all the people you loved were

Quick to turn their backs

When you feel your soul callusing beyond healing

To the point it don't matter

When I realized my nonchalant mood after the
Bryant tragedy

Is when I finally accepted

I have been transformed into a man incapable of
feeling

I guess that's expected after giving so much of it
away

Now it's gone

I'm glad

I'm incapable of feeling.

GOD DON'T LIVE HERE

Where we gotta run when police hit the corner

No gun on your hip equals another South Central
Murder

Why every day I have to juggle

My funeral or prison

No insurance or victims of crimes if I get shot

Can't say, if LAPD catch me with it

Or my mama on news, crying because of unfair
verdict

I'm talking about if the crooked officers were to

Be put on trial for the unfair murder of her child

Where news manipulates black slayings as just

Another evil thing

Tell me, who really lives here?

SOULS MEET

I wonder, will we ever link again

Do these kinda things really happen

Or only in the end, or only in those scenes where

Writers script it in

When I think of such

I think of something like souls racing on clouds

Shining to the point of no return

I picture smiles bright as light, this ain't no dream,

I said

I must be high

We meet again

This time

It feels like

We are high in the sky.

DEAR BG

I can't lie

I'm kinda fucked up

I never knew one thing could mean so much to
me

Truthfully, I can't explain how something so foul

Could mean so much to me

We been through so much you and me

I never envisioned the day we would split

I can't believe this shit

This whole time you been a cold-hearted bitch

You turn on me every chance you get

Honestly, how can I trip

Just like life

This one street

Brynhurst Ave. aka BG

That treacherous avenue

Is colder than a bitch.

LETTER TO MOMS

Instead of saying something like

You act just like yha dead-beat dad

How about something like

Son, you can still be Obama

I don't mean no harm

Just because I'm from a murderous street gang

Don't mean I never missed the guidance and

Presence of my mama

Hopefully one day, hopefully

You will come around.

WILLIE LYNCH SYNDROME

When blacks encounter opposite race

The tone is sincere with greetings of a good morning

Black man come face 2 face with his same race

Followed is another black ghetto family mourning

Plan has gone greater than the masses expected

No need for KKK

We just gone continue to play

On these dumb niggas' ignorance

No need to wonder why there's a decrease in

Black faces in South Los Angeles

Now let me get back to perpetrating on Instagram

Is what the blacks do

Like their life is full of riches and everything is just fine.

RICH

Picture my community

Rich abundance of unity

Prison shackled stolen from land *1619* plan

Remove from stolen grounds *2020* plan

Hit ground *Nigga*

Shoot if you make sound *Nigga*

My ancestors blood still stain the same brown soil

Congress use Hispanics to plow

Nobody cares about another black boy laid dead
on the corner

The white man pointed out to the Chinese

Space for another liquor store

The real plan is

Buy all big mama houses, send Section-8 out

Before the Mayflower, the plan has been

Remove from their promised land

African Americans die broke, robbed riches

Indebted slaves on his stolen land

Too dumb to understand

Niggers

Is what they really call us.

YOUR HEART

I wish I'd realized from the start

It gotta come from the heart

It's not formatted correctly nor comes with

Instructions, It's from the heart

I've come to learn

It never works

Unless it's coming from the heart

How so

If it's true

You can strike it in the dark

I finally realize

True poetry

It gotta come from the heart.

BIG BUSINESS

Big steel truck just pulled in

Procession of the black family just rolled out

I wonder how many black bodies it take to get

Promoted in the KKK

It don't even matter, my homies have switched

Positions

All this hate I can't help but to think

The 77th division got the highest percentage in

Unarmed black killings

Nobody care, they're trying to extinct us

I figured their plot out

While sitting in the grass at Inglewood Cemetery

Right after I saw that same federal reserve truck

Banking the corner full leaving out.

THESE STREETS

I'm standing with all my friends

Why do I feel energy like I'm surrounded by a circle of enemies?

I sense the envy when you look at me

I feel it in their handshakes

Hugs that come with not enough weight in their embrace

Smiles not matching what he or she say

The truth is always smeared across everyone's face

What other vibe I'm supposed to get

When you grew up in a land existence defined by

Catching bodies, no matter if caught on tape

How I'm wondering why he was killed by a friend he'd known since

Age eight

I'm talking about the land of no friends, AKA the

Treacherous Rollin 60s

Where you get killed or go to jail before having sex

I spent my adolescent years burying kids

Their precious brains and blood still stain these LA streets.

THE PLAN

They killing us

Operation "Replace solid wit niggas compromising"

These women been poisoning their kids' brains

Filling their small heads with toxins more deadly

Than lead

That man used to murder his childhood friend

Why I wonder how all my homies come up dead

Police recorded this as just another rival dead

He was standing next to an alleged friend

The way most of my homies come up dead.

THE GANG

Gunshot to his brain

The mother who feels the pain

A celebration that brings out everybody in
the rain

All in the name of the gang

Average souls can't endure this pain

All in the name of my gang

A white once spoke these words one day

The black race is insane

How can we be mad about these chains
from

Back in the day?

Or how we treated Kunta Kinte

We doing the same

In the name of our gang.

ONE

That's all it takes to get life

Less than that when it's time to die

The only thing you can't rewind

The number of the woman you can't replace

It takes less than this just to think

You cannot duplicate

If you had sixty seconds to think

How much time would you take

It takes less than this just to think.

THEY WONDER WHY

Why we scream, "Fuck the police"

Why you always fucking with me

Why you always racial profiling me

What's supposed to be a place of peace you turn

Into a chaotic scene

You are one of the reasons why I keep a gun on me

Why you got your nine trained on me

You wonder why we can't stand you police

We see the hate in your red face

That's why we scream, "Fuck the police"

It will never be equality

That's why I scream "Fuck the police."

NOBODY

These youngins out here catching bodies

No fear in everyone lurking these streets

It's all about that homicide

Who can make a mama cry

Over six shots to my driver side

What if I died

Just another untapped potential dead

I was laying with four holes in that hospital bed

Nobody is exempt

When bullets hit yha head

Do it really matter what your nickname was

You nobody at the end

Another body laid on that metal slab

Hopefully

Not another nigga

That another was killed in the field at the end.

TINY SWEEZE AND CP

It's kinda hard to speak on this in the opening

I remember both of y'all caskets open at the viewings

It's sad

My young niggas didn't get the chance to see their light
shine

Never got the chance to experience what a real hoe was
like

I remember vividly both them days

Me, Mudroll, and Marquise getting head in the

Back of the building by a fiend

Lil CP was fucking with this female that stayed on

The corner, we called Honey-C

I was right there

Both them days

I was there when them ambulances neared

Almost twenty years later

I still cry about Tiny Sweeze and Lil CP

May these two rest in peace

Raymond and Marquise.

PUBLICITY STUNT

Daps and shoulder hugs

Turn backs it's mean mugs

Passing me that blunt don't mean love

It's hate in that Hennessy cup

A nigga will kill a brother behind Remy

Be draped in jewels but don't got change for a fifty

Claim they more up than you but still waiting to
sneak you

They waiting to pay you in full like Alpo did

Be careful

Of those who put on when the camera on

Especially those that say, "I love you, bro"

Say, "Cheese"

It's all a publicity stunt.

BACK IN THA DAY

Whatever happened to

You really care how my mama doing

Being there for me

I guess them days is over

Remember when we used to wait on each other
after school

Pieced up on weed before a such thing as us
smoking backwoods

I'm talking about them days they reminiscent on

In that movie, *The Wood*

Who would ever knew

You caught life before age twenty-two

Every time I watch *Boyz n the Hood* I think of you

Who would have knew

135

All the things we love would soon disappear

Just like Ice Cube does at the end.

HAMMERS & COKE

Is all I knew growing up

Cutting up rocks like I was in a diamond lab

I carried enough shots for a first-grade class

Them trips to juvenile camp used to have my mama
mad

She refused to visit me in state pen

That's how I ended up in the feds

Officers found two ounces of dope in my kitchen
cabinet

Repercussions of abandonment as a troubled kid

Way before they retrieved the deuce-five I threw over
the gate at

Compers

When I was running from the woman who had my kids

Guns and dope, along with her

Most of what I've been to jail for

I used to think these were the only things I needed

I used to think, all I just said

What was all I had to live for.

CATTLE

You ain't no different from an animal

The mortician butcher you up

Use fluids to embalm you

Served you up, digest you into waist food

No life insurance get your remains treated same as USDA

The aftermath of slaughter is how they create rib eye steak

After prison riots, racist correction officers get hazards pay

Why you think white police get no time after killing unarmed blacks

Equals no justice for blacks, period

Look up the constitution

They view us like lions do herds

In case it ran past you

Meat on their food chain

At least in Africa we roam free

In the United States, if you die broke

Just another piece of unclaimed meat.

South Central Glossary

All-nighter Grinding. Selling drugs from evening until daylight.

Active An aggressive member who's fully involved in gang activities.

Ball To attempt or successfully deceive someone in a clever manner. {You balled me.}

Billy Synonym for firearm/gun. The nickname stems from the famous gunslinger William H. Bonney, a.k.a. "Billy the Kid."

Blood The formal saying/greeting from one Blood to another. In reference to the color red.

Blower In reference to the handgun.

Bumper A large, nicely-shaped buttock.

Bust A Bitch   Making a U-turn abruptly in the middle of
the street.

Buster   The scary one out of the group.

Character   Someone known to behave foolishly.

Chipped   Somebody died. {The homie got chipped
last night, smh.}

Chili   Money: currency.

Citch   In reference to bitch {slang} used by only
Crips.

Craccin   Mainly used by Crips as slang and
articulation of: What's up/to convey the
severity of a situation/a challenge, and not
limited to conflict. A word used by Bloods
as well (What's brackin).

Crash   {Community, revolution, against, street,
Hoodlums.} A squad of police officers
who purposely target gang members.

Crim   Abbreviation of Criminal. Substitution of
                    Groove, used by the Hoovers criminals.

Cuz   Formal saying/greeting from one Crip to
                    another. Thriving from the related word
                    "Cousin".

Dead   In respect to fallen comrades {On the
Homies   Dead Homies}. The slogan is used to
                    validate the severity/truthfulness of said
                    topic or discussion.

Dusty   No money, broke. Dirty dress attire. Bad
                    hygiene. {Girl … Michael is always
                    Dusty!}

Enemigo   The opposing side—the enemy.

Extras   Doing "the most" when uncalled for.

Flipper/Flip   A female who will have sex with a random
                    person short of notice. Or, a person who
                    sleeps with anybody for no monetary gain.
                    Anywhere. Anytime.

Flipped   Being killed. {That boy got flipped last night.}

Foolie/Fool   A greeting used the same as Bro/Brother/Homie.

Fruit Cake   A homosexual.

Fu Fur   Shares the same likeness as "Goofball" and "Mickey." {This dude is a fu fur}.

Function   A party get-together.

Gang Banger   An active hoodlum who participates in all acts surrounding gang activity, and violence, and engages in conflicts with rivals.

Gangster   A distinguished individual who does not hesitate to handle his/her business. Category/group in gang culture, different, in comparison to: Neighborhood Crips, Hoover criminals, and Bloods. Word and term used by such as, not limited to 43

Gangstas, 83 Gangstas, and Denver Lane Gangster Bloods.

Gang Member
A person that belongs and claims a set {Gang—Neighborhood}. Also, an individual gang member, who was once active, has retired to the status of inactive.

Goofball
Another word for lame, corny, an unfavorable person amongst peers. A man who acts like a child.

Ghetto Bird
Helicopter. Thriving from a statistical fact. Police presence is common in surrounding areas of South Central, Los Angeles.

Groove
The formal greeting, slang, and sayings of the Hoover criminals.

Going Up
Indulging in drugs or having sex.

Hammer
Handgun: also coined "A Thumper".

Hood
The abbreviation of neighborhood, is also used to replace the word *Good*. Also used

	as the formal greeting of one Neighborhood Crip to another. {Everything Hood} {Hoodsta Crip} Rollin 40,50,60,90, Neighborhood Crips,
Hook Up	etc.
	A firearm. A term created and used by the Rollin 60s. Slang created in reference to someone needing to be hooked up to an I.V, from penetration of bullets to body.
Hoodsta	A resilient individual with character and honor, who survives in trenches all across the world, known as thy neighborhood. Also: a Hoodsta is known as a distinguished individual with integrity, morals, and honor; deriving from the proper slang term: *Hoodster.*
Jerking	A celebration-function, at its full peak of excitement. {This party is jerkin'.
Johnnie	Code word for police officers; be aware or run when you see law enforcement.

Legend has it, the name stems from a 77th police officer's first name, who had the reputation of chasing down gang members vigorously.

Lick   Robbery. A caper with the promise of producing currency.

Link Up   Meeting up at an agreed-upon time and location.

Loc   Recognition of high honor for a Crip. Slang that's used in the same respect as cuz.

Low ball   This word varies in meaning. A scandalous individual with scavenger tendencies. Or in reference to someone being down on their luck. {I'm low-ballin'.}

Mack in   To make contact, link up, in physical form or verbal.

Mark   Sometimes used in a joking manner but holds the same validity as "Coward".

Mickey   Someone who is considered a "character" or "odd" by his/her peers. A person who exhibits unacceptable behavior.

Off Deck   Someone considered not reliable, not living up to expectations {you off-deck, man}.

Out   of Being caught in rival territory.
Bounds

Passed   Heist, robbery, or successful mission completed.

Played Up   The act of a woman/individual; standing someone up; flaking; being unavailable.

Politicking   Speaking on anyone or controversial topics amongst peers.

Ratchet　　A lascivious female who dresses provocatively. {I like ratchet-ass Tynisha … She always wears tight shorts!}

Rat　　Used to label a female that has a long sexual history; also the term used to defame a person known for telling.

Skull Drag　　To inflict crucial harm upon a human. Basically, to beat someone's ass. {I'm about to skull drag this fool.}

Single　　Cigarettes from the corner stores in urban communities. {Get me two singles from the smoke shop, Newports.}

Slippin'　　Being caught by rivals without a weapon.

Snitch　　A person that divulges volunteer information of any sort to law enforcement agencies that aids in anyone's incarceration; a rat.

Take Down   Meaning, you are about to accomplish a goal. Or, embarking on a sexual endeavor.

The Track   Certain Blvds in LA County where prostitutes and pimps frequent/work.

Third   Slang Crips used to represent the "3"/"3rd". Such as the Avalon Gangster Crips.

Thirsty   An overzealous individual who will do anything to achieve a desired goal, whether petty or honorable.

Toss up   Females who are easy to have sex with {Hey, bro … she's a toss-up}.

Troub   Abbreviation of trouble; greeting; slang adopted by the Trouble Gangster Crips. Close affiliates of the Hoover criminals.

Turnt up   At the max; full of energy; motivated; inspired. {I'm turnt up… let's hit the club!}

Weirdo   The word that is a wobbler—can be hard
                          to discern. It can be taken as disrespect, or
                          a sign of endearment, depending on who
                          the administrator is, and how the wobbler
                          is delivered. {You're weird! You're acting
                          weird.}

With   the   Used as a question, slang, and statement to
Business   validate a person's reputation in high
                          regard. {I had a problem with these two
                          guys yesterday. Mike jumped out of his
                          seat to help me ... he with the business.}

Work   Drugs. Mainly referring to cocaine.

Worked   The act of getting over someone.

Working   Informant for law enforcement, whether
                          being compensated or not.

Yee   Classified the same as "Buster." A term
                          used by West Side Bloods.

Zesty   A male that exhibits suspect behavior in relation to sexuality. An individual unable to differentiate as heterosexual or bisexual.

Author's contact

Website: NFRNDSpublication.com